You Will Soon Bloom

Andrea Lopez

Copyright © Andrea Lopez, 2021

All rights reserved. No part of this book may be used or reproduced in any manner whatsoever without written permission from the author except in the case of brief quotations embodied in critical articles or reviews.

ISBN: 978-1-945649-96-7

This book was made through the Cuentos workshop by Yesika Salgado and Daniel Lisi.

Contents

9	Blank
10	Coffee
11	Sentimiento
12	Wondering
13	Slap
14	Tell Me How You Really Feel
15	Dry
16	3am in Bed
17	Missing You
18	Goodnight Moon
19	Choose Wisely Please.
20	UGOTME
21	BeGone
22	A letter to YOU.
23	Worth it
24	Love You[rself]
25	Ocean Calling
26	"Living"
27	2AM
28	Summer Lover
29	Una Canción de Amor
30	Dream_Boy_
31	Living Daydream
32	What a Woman

You Will Soon Bloom

By Andrea Lopez

Blank

White canvas in front of me.
I can paint this with all the bright colors.
I am an artist, I have the control.
I can press the brush so hard or lightly stroke.
Others watch as I begin to create my piece.
I expect them to critique.
But they won't ruin my peace.
Today is the day I begin on what will be my masterpiece.

Coffee

You're a perfect blend I want to take a sip of.
Seeing you and my days lit up.
You're a tall dark roast of deliciousness.
I can take you hot or cold.
Run through me so smoothly.
I have a highly caffeinated crush on you.
You come towards me, without hesitation.
I can't help but start a conversation.
Now we sit together at the table.
Enjoying the presence of each other.
We say our goodbye as I take my last sip.
Tomorrow it starts all over again.

Sentimiento

Mi español no es muy bueno.
Pero es suficiente para decirte, como me siento.
Cuando te veo, tengo una sonrisa muy grande.
La manera que me vez, sube mi presión de sangre.
Mi corazón empieza a saltar.
No lo puedo calmar.
Cuando hablas conmigo
Mis ojos no pueden alejarse de ti.
Te siguen.
Observando tu posición.
Quiero conocer tu corazón.
Era la manera que caminaste hacia mi lado y te sentaste frente a mi,
que me di cuenta a quien yo quiero es a ti.

Wondering

Can it really be?
That you have an interest in me?
Or am I just too naive?
So quickly to believe.
I'm left wondering.
Extreme overthinking.
About how I am feeling.
I just couldn't stop staring.
You couldn't stop smiling.
Can this be the beginning of something?
Maybe.
You know what they say…
Seeing is believing.

Slap

They say you don't deserve me, that you are not the one.
I don't want to believe them but you keep showing the part.
Why can't I move on? Why do you have a hold on me?
I need to escape, because this can't be my reality.
You had me wrapped around your finger, one call and I was there.
I wanted to help you, not knowing I was hurting myself.
Your spell is wicked, I doubt it can be undone.
I counted you as a friend and now I'm realizing you are failing at being one.

Tell Me How You Really Feel

My friends ask me if I'm okay.
What am I suppose to say?
Yeah I'm fine. Life is great.
Wrong.
The truth is I'm not, and I'm tired of putting up a front.
I'm tired of the fake smiles and laughs.
When in reality, I feel so sad.
The pain is behind the smile, you can't see it.
My heart is torn apart, but you can't feel it.
I wanted him to be mine so bad.
I never was given the chance.
Pain from heartbreak, it hurts so much.
Tears keep falling, I can't keep up.
When will I really be okay?
I don't have an answer.
So I stay quiet and suffer.

Dry

Like a flower,
I want this relationship to grow naturally.
We embedded the seed, watered it daily, and provided the sunlight.
Months past, but still no sign of growth.
I am confused as I see no progress.
Why hasn't it blossomed into its beautiful form?
I'm left blaming myself for this to be happening.
But I shouldn't guilt trip myself, because in the end you were the one damaging.
You let it dry out.
Not even giving us the chance to sprout.
We could've grown into something beautiful.
But in the end, I was not meant to be planted with you.

3am in Bed

I don't know what is going on in my head.
Lately, I have been such a mess.
Been trying to smile more and cry less.
Truth is, you caused me stress.
I needed to address my feelings, but you weren't feeling them.
Crying myself to sleep is the only way I have good dreams.
You lead me on.
Don't tell me you didn't feel this bond.
Hours turn to days.
Days turn into months.
I'm trying to heal but my heart aches so much.

Missing You

Oh how I wish I can see you one more time.
Kiss that wrinkled skin of yours and see that smile shine.
To hear your voice call my name.
To receive a hug from you that is a full force of warmth.
You loved me unconditionally.
Telling me I was your pride and joy.
Always supported me in all that I have done.
I wish you can see
how beautiful I am turning out to be.
Time never stops, but if I could, I would ask God to stop the clock.
Ask him if he can so kindly rewind.
To bring me back to where you and I were in the same lifetime.

Goodnight Moon

I've been taking some time to be alone with myself.
This intimate moment is where I reflect.
It has been therapy for my mental health.
I coat myself with radiance and positivity on the outside.
For I am drained on the inside,
with so much on my mind, trying to find my purpose in life.
I feel like the moon.
Always facing the same way every day of the night
with light to give to you.
But never show the other side,
the cold and dark parts that I try so hard to hide.
On this night, I look at the moon and tell her my worries.
She prays for me, for I tell her I want to be full again.

Choose Wisely Please.

Take a look at me.
Can you love me deeply?
Deeper than what your eyes can see?
I am more than just my skin.
Come and feel my heartbeat.
Do you feel that rhythm?
Love... that is all me.
As confident as I may seem,
I still deal with insecurities.
Bet you've seen prettier flowers than me.
I'm thankful to be in your garden,
but will you pick me?
Or will I be left alongside the weeds...

UGOTME

Thinking of you before I sleep.
I start closing my eyes and you begin to transition into my dreams.
Please don't leave, I want to keep you here with me.
Even when I slumber, you got my mind on a monitor.
Ever since you, I've stopped counting sheep.
My love for you has no capacity.
We love each other in my dreams,
because I doubt you feel the same way in reality.
You're a treasure I never want to give away.
So I ask you one time, can you please stay?

BeGone

It's the same old shit. I'm used to the hurt.
I was rooting for you, but I see you're letting me go.
When will I learn?
I'm tired of feeling so low.
You're breaking my spirit.
This isn't how I'm supposed to be feeling.
All I was doing was showing you love.
But you're lacking at giving a response.
The sun always comes up,
she'll heal me from feeling so blue.
I'm done wilting over you.
I need to focus on my own roots.
For I deserve to bloom.
Let it be known, you won't be in the way of my growth.

A letter to YOU.

Tell me why you're sad.
Let me be the one to comfort you.
In the end, I'm the only one you'll ever have.
You may have others that you call your best friend,
but I got you till the end.

Tell me why you're happy.
I like seeing you glow.
I know certain things make you feel sappy.
C'mon tell me, I wanna know.

Tell me why you're angry.
I know life can be frustrating.
Don't blame yourself, I see that you are trying.
I want you to succeed, let me be your right hand.
Catch me cheering you on in the stands.
You know I'm always going to be your biggest fan.

Worth it

Look at who I'm becoming.
The old me would never believe that she was capable of doing all these amazing things.
But look at me.
I was guided by my heart, telling me that I can be so much more.
"Know your self worth"
But let me be clear, I've fallen and been hurt.
However, I've been turning my tears into words.
Sharing my words for other girls to hear.
To help them know they too are worthy.
Worthy of being able to grow into someone they adore.

Love You[rself]

I don't think I tell you this enough.
You deserve to hear this everyday.
I just want to say, how thankful I am for you.
Thank you for loving me the way I am.
You have seen me at my best
and even on the days when I'm a mess.
You love me so well, even with my flaws.
When I see you, I'm in awe.
I know I take you for granted at times and it should stop.
For you deserve to be treated like the queen you are.

Ocean Calling

I hear the waves coming in.
My soul is asking for a cleanse.
I need the water to rinse away all the hurt I have been feeling.
I take a step in, making my way into the deep.
Feeling the body of water moving me.
The waves are getting stronger.
Getting past them is a struggle.
The current is only for a moment.
After the hardship, comes the calmness.
I open my arms; I bring my body up to the surface.
Floating in the ocean. I hear nothing but silence.
The rays of sunlight hitting my body.
I'm thankful for this moment.

"Living"

I wake up to kisses from the sun.
I'm nothing but an earthling.
I thank the Lord that I am breathing.
There is no use in being angry.
I'm just trying to enjoy this thing called "living".
I'm attracted to your nature.
If I have love to give, I will give it.
Don't you try to suppress me.
Let me shower you flowers.
Walk toward the beach & enjoy the sunset hour.
Look at how pretty the sky glows.
The moon gets ready to brighten the night.
When I'm done with this life.
Meet me out in the wild.
I'll be enjoying the African breeze.
Being the animal I always wanted to be.

2AM

I need to be honest with you.
No more hiding these feelings.
It's just me and you, let me talk to you for a minute.
You have beauty like no other.
My heart has grown fonder for you.
Please tell me that you see me.
I just want to love you wholeheartedly.
Through your glory and gloomy days, can I be there
for you every step of the way?
Please tell me, you see me.
Do you feel the same way too?
My heart has been yearning for yours.
If need be, I'll wait for you patiently.
All I ask is that you don't mislead me.
I don't want my heart to hurt.

Summer Lover

I see him from a distance, I'm calling out his name.
I hope that he is listening to the messages I have sent.
His mind is so intriguing,
I'm curious to know his reasons.
Skin just like the summer season,
I admire his natural glow.
Young boy with an old soul,
I enjoy seeing his growth.
My admiration grows larger every time he prospers.
I don't know how we crossed paths, but I'm thankful to God that we did.

Una Canción de Amor

Te dedico una canción, espero que la escuches.
La puedo oír seguido porque cada vez que la escucho,
tú imagen entra en mi mente.
Te dedico esta canción.
Cuando toca, siento mucha emoción.
Pienso en tu energía, tú eres la razón de mi alegría.
Perdón por mi manera de ser tímida.
Me toma tiempo para confesar,
el amor que te quiero dar.
Por favor escucha la canción,
de la dedicó a ti, porque tú eres un amor para mi.

Dream_Boy_

Boy I be having dreams about you.
I'm really out here thanking God, for putting us underneath the same moon.
I'm so swoon over you.
Gotta admit your vocabulary is pretty smooth.
Smooth, just like that hair of yours that I wanna run my fingers through.
Meet me underneath the cotton candy sky,
I'm down for a photoshoot.
My focus is all on you.
No need to worry,
I understand you value loyalty.
You say you need time.
I have all the patience.
You place your hand over mine, tell me boy, what is your heart saying?

Living Daydream

As you can see,
it's hard for me to confess my feelings.
That's why I write poetry.
It's easier for me to write what I feel.
I hope you read them.
It's you who I think about, when my pen meets the paper.
Every piece has a piece of you.
Without you, there is no flavor.
You're a living daydream.
The only one that I see.
Always running through my mind.
You're the perfect mixture of reality & fantasy.
Oh, what a beautiful being.

What a Woman

Oh baby girl, you look so fine. Your skin is glowing, you're shining so bright.
You have conquered through so much.
Love, heartache, and lost.
You kept on going, even on the days you wanted to give up.
Some days were harder, where you just wanted to drop dead.
But you didn't let yourself fall.
You are a mighty woman, with an energy that has so many in awe.
Keep growing, you know you're only getting stronger.
You deserve a cheer, for you didn't let your fears get the best of you.
I can't wait to see *our* beauty evolve this year.

Andrea Lopez has been writing poetry for over two years. Ever since she was little her favorite hobby was reading. Fascinated with books, she decided to start writing short stories at the age of thirteen. As she got older she discovered her love for poetry after reading Reyna Biddy's *I Love My Love*. Writers like Reyna Biddy, Yesika Salgado, and Nayyirah Waheed gave Andrea a spark inside her to start sharing her poems among friends and eventually have the public to see. Andrea hopes that those who read her poems can sense her transparency and find an emotional connection to them.

www.ingramcontent.com/pod-product-compliance
Lightning Source LLC
Chambersburg PA
CBHW030203100526
44592CB00009B/419